Pearson Baccalaureate PYP Readers

Camping

Sarah Russell

Going camping

Last summer, I went camping with my family. We spent two nights in the countryside.

There were no houses where we stayed.
Can you guess what we did?

Pitching a tent

We stayed in a tent.
We **pitched** the tent and slept in it.

There were no shops where we stayed.
What did we eat?
How did we cook our food?

Cooking

We took all the food we needed with us. We also took our **cooking equipment**. We cooked outside.

There were no beds in our tent. *Can you guess what we slept in?*

Sleeping

We took sleeping bags to sleep in. We put them on the ground inside the tent.
Have you slept in a sleeping bag?

There was no **electricity** in our tent.
How did we see at night?

In the dark

We took a **torch** to help us see in the dark. It was fun using the torch in the dark.

Can you remember everything we took with us?

Equipment

tent

torch

sleeping bag

camping stove

Can you remember what we used these things for?

Our camping trip

First we pitched our tent.

Then we cooked our food.

At night we slept in our sleeping bags.

We had lots of fun!

Glossary

cooking equipment everything needed to cook food

electricity power used for lights and cooking

pitched put up a tent and set it firmly on the ground

torch a light powered by batteries

Index